I0436618

YAKALOU MEDIA

GET CLARITY ABOUT YOUR DECISION-MAKING PROCESS

100 Questions To Ask Yourself To Learn How To Make Better Decisions In Your Life

Contents

Disclaimer

This book is designed to provide information only. This information is provided and sold with the knowledge that the publisher and author do not offer any legal or other professional advice. In the case of a need for any such expertise, consult with the appropriate professional.

This book does not contain all the information available on the subject. This book has not been created to be specific to any individual's or organization's situation or needs. Every effort has been made to make this book as accurate as possible. However, there may be typographical and/or content errors. Therefore, this book should serve only as a general guide, not as the ultimate source of subject information.

This book contains information that might be dated and is intended only to educate and entertain. Regarding any loss or damage allegedly suffered or alleged to have occurred as a result of the information in this book, either directly or indirectly, the author and publisher shall have no liability or responsibility to any person or entity.

Introduction

Have you ever wondered why some decisions seem effortless while others feel like a maze with no clear exit? Welcome to "Get Clarity About Your Decision-Making Process," a guide designed to unravel the complexities of choices we face daily. The purpose of this book is straightforward yet powerful: to provide you with a set of practical tools and questions that illuminate the path to better decision-making.

Why is effective decision-making so crucial, you might ask? Well, think about it. Our lives are essentially the sum of the decisions we make. From the small choices like what to eat for breakfast to the significant ones like choosing a career path or a life partner, each decision shapes our journey. But how often do we pause to reflect on the process behind these decisions? Are we making choices based on well-thought-out reasons, or are we simply reacting to what's in front of us?

This book is here to help you delve into these questions. It's designed to be your companion in uncovering the hidden factors that influence your decisions. We'll explore how your values and emotions play a role, how past experiences can be a treasure trove of lessons, and how understanding your goals can light up your decision-making path. With each chapter, you'll find yourself equipped with sharper tools to cut through the fog of indecision and confusion.

Our journey will not just be about making decisions but also about making them confidently and wisely. Have you ever made a decision only to later experience doubt? This book aims to minimize that uncertainty. By the end, you'll not only be making decisions more efficiently, but you'll also gain a deeper understanding of yourself, your goals, and how to navigate the unpredictable waters of life with newfound confidence.

So, are you ready to embark on this journey of transformation? Are you prepared to unlock the secrets of effective decision-making that can lead you to a more fulfilling life? Let's turn the page and start this enlightening adventure together.

The 5 Rules to Get the Most Out of This Book

As you embark on the journey through this book, it's essential to approach it with an open mind and a willingness to engage deeply. To maximize the benefits of this guide, there are five simple yet impactful rules to follow. These rules are designed not just to guide you through the book but to transform your experience into a journey of personal growth and improved decision-making.

Rule 1: Be Open to Self-Reflection

The journey to better decision-making begins with introspection. As you navigate through each chapter, be prepared to ask yourself tough questions and be honest in your answers. Remember, this is a safe space for self-discovery. Are you ready to look inward and explore your true motivations, fears, and desires?

Your Journey - Making This Book Work for You

Welcome to a unique journey with this book—a journey where the path you take is as individual as you are. You might be wondering if you need to read every page, cover to cover, to reap the benefits. The answer is a resounding no. This book is designed to be flexible, allowing you to jump to sections or questions that resonate with your current needs and feelings. It's about making this experience truly yours.

Let's begin by acknowledging that everyone's journey in decision-making is different. Your challenges and dilemmas are unique to your life's context. This book, therefore, is not a linear path but a spectrum of insights and tools. You have the freedom to navigate this resource in a way that aligns with your current situation. Are you grappling with a tough decision right now? Or are you looking to enhance your overall decision-making skills for the future? The structure of this book supports both these needs and everything in between.

Imagine this book as a map. Just as a traveler might focus on different parts of a map depending on their destination, you can focus on different parts of this book based on your current decision-making needs. Each chapter and question is a landmark in the landscape of decision-making. You might find yourself drawn to the chapter on 'Understanding Your Values' during a period of self-reflection or 'Dealing with Uncertainty' when facing a particularly unpredictable choice.

This flexible approach has another significant advantage: it keeps the content fresh and relevant. Each time you come back to a chapter or a question, you bring new experiences and perspectives, making the insights you gain even more profound. Think of it as visiting a familiar place at different times of the year; each visit brings a new perspective and a different experience.

The chapters in this book are crafted with both simplicity and depth. You'll find that each segment offers immediate value, whether it's a quick insight from a single question or a more profound understanding from reading an entire chapter. The structure is designed to cater to both moments when you need quick guidance and times when you're seeking in-depth exploration.

Consider, too, the practical exercises sprinkled throughout the book. These are your tools for active engagement with your decision-making process. They can be revisited as many times as needed, each time offering a new layer of understanding or a different angle to approach your decisions.

In essence, this book is your companion in the journey of decision-making. It's a resource you can turn to time and again, in different moments and for various needs. Whether you read it page by page or jump directly to sections that speak to you at the moment, the wisdom and guidance within these pages remain accessible and relevant.

So, as you continue with this book, remember that your journey through it is yours to define. There is no right or wrong way to navigate these pages. Each path you choose is valid and valuable. Embrace this journey with an open heart and a curious mind, and discover the many ways in which this book can enrich your decision-making journey.

Chapter 1: Understanding Your Values

Meet Emily, a software developer who recently faced a career crossroads. She was offered a high-paying job at a prestigious tech firm, a dream for many in her field. Yet she hesitated. Why? Because Emily had another passion: community work, something the new job wouldn't leave time for. This dilemma brought her face-to-face with a crucial aspect of decision-making: understanding personal values.

Like Emily, many of us encounter situations where our choices reflect our core values. But what are these values? Simply put, they are the principles and beliefs that guide our actions and give meaning to our lives. They are the silent forces behind our decisions, big and small. Recognizing and understanding these values is like having a compass in the complex journey of life.

So, how do you begin to understand and define your own values? Start by looking at the decisions you've made. What do they say about what's important to you? Think about the times you felt most fulfilled. What were you doing? Who were you with? Reflecting on these moments can offer significant insights into your core values.

Now, consider the opposite—situations that made you uncomfortable or unhappy. Often, these are instances where your values are challenged or neglected. Understanding what doesn't sit well with you is just as important as knowing what does. It's through this process of introspection and reflection that you can start to paint a clearer picture of your personal value system.

But why is this important for decision-making? Knowing your values acts as a filter through which you can assess your options. It ensures that your decisions align with what truly matters to you, leading to more satisfaction and less regret.

As you turn the pages of this chapter, think of Emily and her choice. She eventually turned down the lucrative job offer to pursue a balance of her tech career and community work. Why? Because she understood her values of contribution and balance were more important than the prestige and money of the new job.

Now, it's your turn to explore your values. Here are 10 straight-forward questions to help you delve deeper:

1. What moments in life brought you immense joy, and why?
2. Recall a time you were deeply upset. What value was being challenged?
3. What activities make you lose track of time?
4. Think of a person you admire greatly. What qualities of theirs do you value?
5. What are three things you couldn't imagine your life without?
6. When do you feel most like yourself?
7. Imagine your perfect day. What elements are present in it?
8. What causes or issues do you feel most passionate about?
9. If you had all the money in the world, how would you choose to spend your time?
10. What legacy do you want to leave behind?

As you engage with these questions and the exercise, remember that understanding your values is not a one-time task but an evolving process. Let this chapter be the starting point of a journey to deeper self-awareness and more purposeful decision-making.

Exercise #1

Practical Exercise:

Create a 'Values Vision Board'. Collect images, quotes, and items that resonate with your values and arrange them on a board or digital platform. This visual representation of your values will serve as a constant reminder and guide in your decision-making journey.

Chapter 2: Recognizing Emotions

Josh, a seasoned manager, had always prided himself on his logical, data-driven decision-making skills. But one day, he made a hasty decision to reprimand an employee publicly. Later, he realized his action was more a result of his frustration over an unrelated personal issue than the employee's minor mistake. This incident made Josh confront an often-overlooked aspect of decision-making: the influence of emotions.

Emotions, whether we acknowledge them or not, play a significant role in our decision-making process. They can be subtle guides or powerful drivers, influencing our choices. Recognizing and understanding these emotional influences is critical for making balanced and sound decisions.

How do we tell the difference between a choice that is based on fleeting emotions and one that is sound reasoning? The first step is to become aware of our emotional state. Are you feeling stressed, angry, happy, or sad? Acknowledging your emotions is not about letting them dictate your decisions, but rather understanding their impact and adjusting your decision-making process accordingly.

Consider times when you've made impulsive decisions. How were your emotions involved? On the flip side, think about the decisions you made when you were calm and collected. Were the outcomes different? These reflections can reveal how emotions have shaped your choices in the past.

It's also important to recognize that emotions aren't just internal. They can be triggered by people around us or situations we encounter. Understanding this external influence can help us create a buffer, allowing time and space to respond rather than react.

As you explore this chapter, think back to Josh's story. His journey to acknowledge the role of emotions in his decision-making process improved not only his management skills but also his self-awareness. This chapter is designed to guide you through a similar journey of discovery and understanding.

To help you delve deeper, here are some questions to consider:

1. Recall a decision you regret. What emotions were you experiencing at the time?
2. Think of a decision you're proud of. Were your emotions different compared to the regretful decision?
3. How do you typically respond to stress? Does it affect your decision-making process?
4. Identify a time when someone else's emotions influenced your decision. How did you feel about it afterward?
5. What strategies have you used to calm yourself when making an important decision?
6. Can you think of a situation where recognizing your emotions led to a better decision?
7. How do you differentiate between a gut feeling and an emotional reaction?
8. In what ways have positive emotions influenced your decisions?

9. Do you find it easy or challenging to make decisions when you're emotionally charged? Why?
10. How do external factors like people or environments affect your emotional state when making decisions?

Remember, the goal of this chapter is not to eliminate emotions from the decision-making process but to recognize and understand their influence. By doing so, you'll be better equipped to make decisions that are not only smart but also emotionally intelligent.

Exercise #2

Practical Exercise:

For the next week, keep an emotion journal. Every time you make a significant decision, jot down the emotions you're feeling. Review the journal at the end of the week to observe patterns in how your emotions influence your decision-making.

Chapter 3: Analyzing Past Decisions

Meet Sara, a graphic designer who once turned down a high-profile job offer to stay with a smaller, more familiar company. Years later, she wondered if she had made the right choice. This reflection on a pivotal moment in her past opened up a vital aspect of decision-making: learning from past choices.

Every decision we make, whether it seems successful or not, offers a wealth of insights into our decision-making process. Analyzing these past decisions helps us understand our patterns, biases, and areas where we can improve. But how do we objectively evaluate decisions that are already in the rear-view mirror?

The key lies in stepping back and examining these choices without self-judgment. Consider both the decisions that you're proud of and those that you regret. What led to these decisions? Were there external pressures or internal motivations at play? Understanding the context and factors that influenced your past choices is crucial.

Just like Sara, who realized that her fear of change influenced her job decision, this chapter encourages you to dive into your own history of decisions. It's not about dwelling on the past, but about learning from it to enhance your future decision-making.

To guide you on this introspective journey, here are some questions to ponder:

1. Think of a decision you regret. What would you do differently now?
2. Recall a decision that had a positive outcome. What factors contributed to its success?
3. Have you ever made a decision against your intuition? How did it turn out?
4. Identify a time when peer pressure influenced your decision. Would you handle it differently today?
5. What is a common theme in the decisions you are proud of?
6. Reflect on a snap decision you made. What was the result, and what did you learn from it?
7. How has your decision-making process evolved over the years?
8. Can you identify any recurring patterns in your past decisions?
9. Think of a major decision you made impulsively. What were the consequences?
10. How have your values and priorities influenced your past decisions?

As you work through these questions and the exercise, remember that the goal is not to criticize past choices but to understand and learn from them. Like Sara, you might discover underlying reasons for your decisions that can enlighten and guide your future choices. This chapter is about turning hindsight into a powerful tool for better decision-making.

Exercise #3

Practical Exercise:

Create a 'Decision Timeline'. Map out the significant decisions you've made over the past five years. Next to each, note the outcome and any lessons learned. This visual exercise will help you see patterns and growth in your decision-making journey.

Chapter 4: Setting Goals and Priorities

David, a small business owner, always seemed to be in a constant battle with time. There were never enough hours in the day to accomplish everything he wanted. This changed when he attended a workshop that focused on setting clear goals and priorities. David learned that, without defining what truly mattered, he was merely spinning his wheels.

Like David, many of us struggle with prioritizing because we haven't clearly defined our objectives. Setting goals and establishing priorities is not just about making a to-do list; it's about clarifying what is most important in our lives and aligning our actions with these values.

But how do we begin to set these goals and decide what takes precedence? It starts with introspection. What are your long-term aspirations? What brings you the most satisfaction and fulfillment? Understanding these aspects can guide you in setting meaningful goals and priorities.

This process also involves recognizing that not everything can be a top priority. It's about making conscious choices and being okay with the fact that some things might need to take a backseat. This clarity helps you make decisions that are more aligned with your true objectives.

As you read through this chapter, think of David and his

journey from feeling constantly overwhelmed to being more focused and productive. This transformation began with the simple yet profound act of setting clear goals and understanding his priorities.

To help you in this process of clarification, here are some questions to contemplate:

1. What are the top three goals you want to achieve this year?
2. Reflect on a day last week. How did your activities align with your goals?
3. What tasks or activities do you find yourself consistently putting off?
4. Identify something you spend a lot of time on. Does it contribute to your long-term goals?
5. What are you willing to sacrifice to achieve your priorities?
6. How do you deal with distractions that conflict with your priorities?
7. What steps can you take to make your goals more attainable?
8. How do your goals reflect your personal values?
9. When setting goals, how do you ensure they are realistic and achievable?
10. How do you balance short-term needs with long-term objectives?

Remember, like David, the journey to effective goal-setting and prioritizing is unique to each individual. This chapter is designed to guide you in finding clarity in your objectives, helping you make decisions that are not just reactive but proactive and purposeful.

Exercise #4

Practical Exercise:

Construct a 'Goal Pyramid'. On the base, write your long-term aspirations. In the middle, place your medium-term objectives. At the top, note down immediate actions. This pyramid will help you visualize how daily actions build toward your ultimate goals.

Chapter 5: Evaluating Risks and Benefits

Anna, a financial advisor, was well-versed in weighing risks and rewards for her clients. However, when it came to her personal life, she found it challenging to apply the same principles, especially when faced with the decision to move abroad for a new job opportunity. Her story highlights a critical aspect of decision-making: balancing the pros and cons to assess potential outcomes.

Just like Anna, we often find ourselves at a crossroads where the right choice isn't immediately clear. Evaluating the risks and benefits is a fundamental step in making informed decisions. It involves looking beyond immediate gratification and considering the long-term implications of our choices.

But how do we effectively weigh these pros and cons? It begins with listing out all possible outcomes, both good and bad. This exercise requires honesty and foresight. What are the potential benefits of the decision? What risks are involved? Are there any possible unintended consequences?

This process also involves understanding that no decision is without risk. The key is to find a balance where the potential benefits outweigh the risks, in line with your values and goals.

As you delve into this chapter, remember Anna's journey. She had to carefully consider both the professional growth the new job offered and the personal sacrifices it entailed, like being away from family.

To aid you in this crucial aspect of decision-making, consider these questions:

1. What are the best possible outcomes of the decision you're considering?
2. What are the potential risks or downsides?
3. How do these pros and cons align with your long-term goals?
4. Are there any possible outcomes you haven't considered yet?
5. How would this decision impact your personal life?
6. What is the worst-case scenario, and how likely is it to happen?
7. Can the potential benefits be achieved in other ways with fewer risks?
8. How much does fear of the unknown play into your evaluation of risks?
9. What would be the impact of not making this decision at all?
10. How comfortable are you with the level of risk involved?

In this chapter, as you work through the exercise and questions, you'll learn to apply the same careful consideration as Anna, enabling you to make decisions that are not just safe but also rewarding and aligned with your overall life plan.

Exercise #5

Practical Exercise:

Create a 'Risk-Benefit Analysis' chart for a significant decision you're currently facing. List all possible benefits in one column and all potential risks in another. This visual comparison will assist in making a more balanced and informed decision.

Chapter 6: Seeking Advice and Perspectives

Consider the story of Leo, a young entrepreneur ready to expand his business. Faced with several growth strategies, he felt overwhelmed by the choices. That's when he decided to seek advice from experienced mentors and peers. This step opened up a world of perspectives he hadn't considered and ultimately led him to make a well-informed decision. Leo's experience underlines a valuable aspect of decision-making: the importance of seeking external opinions and perspectives.

In our journey of making decisions, it's easy to get trapped in our own thoughts and biases. Seeking advice from others not only broadens our perspective but also introduces us to insights and experiences we may not possess. But how do we ensure that we're getting valuable advice and not just noise?

It starts with identifying the right people to consult. Who has experience or expertise in the area you're dealing with? Remember, the goal is not to find someone who will make the decision for you, but to provide insights that will help you make a better decision.

As you explore this chapter, think about how Leo's decision could have been narrower without the input from his mentors. This narrative will guide you in appreciating and effectively utilizing external advice in your decision-making process.

To help you harness the value of external opinions, here are some thought-provoking questions:

1. Who in your network has experience or expertise relevant to your decision?
2. How can you differentiate between constructive advice and mere opinion?
3. Have you ever changed a decision based on someone else's insight? How did it turn out?
4. In what situations do you find it most valuable to seek external perspectives?
5. How do you balance conflicting advice from different sources?
6. What steps do you take to ensure you're not just seeking advice that aligns with your preconceptions?
7. How do you maintain your own decision-making autonomy when seeking advice?
8. What have you learned from past experiences where you either ignored or followed external advice?
9. How do external perspectives help you see blind spots in your decision-making?
10. How do you plan to incorporate external advice into your future decision-making?

In this chapter, as you engage with these questions and the exercise, you'll learn to navigate the process of seeking and integrating advice, much like Leo. This approach will enrich your decision-making process, making it more robust and well-rounded.

Exercise #6

Practical Exercise:

For your next significant decision, organize a 'Perspective Gathering Session'. Invite a small group of trusted individuals with diverse backgrounds to discuss your decision. Note down their perspectives, and later, reflect on how these insights add to your understanding of the decision at hand.

Chapter 7: Dealing with Uncertainty

Meet Maya, a graphic designer who was offered two very different job opportunities at the same time. One was a safe, well-paying position with a large corporation; the other was a risky startup with the potential for creative freedom. The uncertainty of each option paralyzed Maya, who was unable to make a choice. Her situation highlights a common challenge in decision-making: handling indecision and managing unclear situations.

Uncertainty is an inevitable part of life, and how we deal with it can significantly impact the course of our personal and professional paths. The key to managing uncertainty is not to eliminate it—that's often impossible—but to develop strategies to navigate through it effectively.

But how does one make decisions when the outcomes are so unclear? The first step is to accept that uncertainty is a natural part of decision-making. It's about learning to be comfortable with not having all the answers and making the best decision with the information available.

As you read through this chapter, consider Maya's dilemma. By accepting the uncertainty and evaluating each option's potential, she was able to make a more informed and confident decision.

To assist you in navigating through uncertain situations, here are some guiding questions:

1. When faced with uncertainty, what are your initial reactions?
2. How do you gather information to make informed decisions in uncertain situations?
3. Can you recall a time when you made a decision despite not having all the details? How did it turn out?
4. What strategies do you use to weigh the unknowns in a decision?
5. How do you deal with the anxiety or stress that comes with uncertain choices?
6. In what ways can embracing uncertainty be beneficial to decision-making?
7. How do you prioritize different factors when outcomes are unclear?
8. What role does intuition play in your decision-making under uncertainty?
9. How do you assess the risks involved in uncertain situations?
10. How do you prepare for unexpected outcomes after making a decision?

In this chapter, you will learn, like Maya, to see uncertainty not as a barrier but as an integral part of the decision-making process. This perspective can transform indecision into a path for growth and better choices.

Exercise #7

Practical Exercise:

Create an 'Uncertainty Map' for the current decision you're facing. List the knowns and unknowns, and for each unknown, brainstorm possible outcomes and how you might handle them. This exercise can help you visualize and prepare for different scenarios, making the uncertainty more manageable.

Chapter 8: Improving Problem-Solving Skills

Jake, an engineer, was known for his methodical approach to problems at work. However, when it came to more personal decisions, like choosing a new home or planning a career change, he found it difficult to apply the same level of analytical thinking. This disconnect highlights an essential skill in decision-making: enhancing your problem-solving abilities.

Problem-solving skills are crucial to making effective decisions. They allow you to dissect a problem, understand its components, and come up with possible solutions. But how does one translate these skills from professional scenarios to personal life decisions?

The answer lies in consciously applying analytical thinking to all areas of life. It involves breaking down a decision into smaller, more manageable parts, assessing each part systematically, and considering various solutions before choosing the best course of action.

As you go through this chapter, think of Jake and his journey to apply his problem-solving skills beyond his engineering projects. This shift not only improved his personal decision-making but also brought a new level of clarity to his choices.

To help enhance your problem-solving skills, here are some questions to ponder:

1. When faced with a problem, what is your initial step in finding a solution?
2. How do you break down complex decisions into smaller, more manageable parts?
3. Can you recall a situation where you successfully applied analytical thinking to a personal decision? What was the outcome?
4. What tools or methods do you use to analyze different aspects of a problem?
5. How do you ensure that your problem-solving approach is comprehensive and considers all possible angles?
6. How do you deal with conflicting information or opinions when solving a problem?
7. What strategies do you use to avoid jumping to conclusions too quickly?
8. How do you avoid letting unrelated issues divert your attention from the current problem?
9. In what ways do you gather and evaluate evidence before making a decision?
10. How do you balance intuition and analytical thinking in your decision-making process?

By the end of this chapter, you will have learned to approach decision-making with the same level of scrutiny and analysis as Jake, enabling more structured, thoughtful, and effective solutions to the challenges you face.

Exercise #8

Practical Exercise:

Engage in a 'Problem-Solving Drill'. Take a recent decision you struggled with and break it down into its core components. Analyze each component, list potential solutions, and evaluate their pros and cons. This exercise will help you sharpen your analytical skills and apply them to various situations.

Chapter 9: Building Confidence in Decisions

Meet Nina, a marketing executive who often second-guesses her decisions, regardless of the outcome. This lack of confidence stemmed not from her inability to make decisions but from a fear of making the wrong ones. Nina's story underscores a crucial aspect of decision-making: building confidence and self-assurance in the choices we make.

Having confidence in our decisions is as important as the process of making them. But how do we build this confidence, especially when past decisions may not have always gone as planned? It starts with understanding that no decision is perfect and that each choice is a step toward learning and growth.

As you delve into this chapter, consider Nina's journey to gaining confidence. She learned to view each decision as a learning opportunity, allowing her to build trust in her judgment over time.

To aid you in boosting your decision-making confidence, here are some insightful questions:

1. Reflect on a decision you made that had a positive outcome. What factors contributed to its success?

2. Think of a time when a decision didn't go as planned. What did you learn from that experience?

3. How do you handle the fear of making the wrong decision?

4. What steps can you take to feel more prepared and informed before making a decision?

5. How do you validate your decisions once they are made?

6. What role does seeking feedback play in your decision-making process?

7. How can you use past successes to boost your confidence in future decisions?

8. In what ways can you remind yourself of your decision-making strengths?

9. How do you deal with external criticism or doubt about your decisions?

10. What strategies can you employ to stay committed to your decision, even when facing uncertainty or challenges?

Through this chapter, much like Nina, you will discover ways to build and maintain confidence in your decision-making. This newfound self-assurance will not only empower your choices but also transform the way you approach future decisions.

Exercise #9

Practical Exercise:

Create a 'Confidence Journal'. Every time you make a decision, big or small, write it down in the journal along with the outcome. Regularly review this journal to remind yourself of the successful decisions you've made and the lessons learned from the less successful ones.

Chapter 10: Long-Term Planning and Impact

Consider the story of Alex, a community leader who spearheaded a project to create a local park. While the initial focus was on the immediate benefits, Alex soon realized the importance of considering the long-term impact of this development on the community. This foresight led to more sustainable and inclusive planning. Alex's experience illustrates a vital element in decision-making: understanding and considering the long-term effects and consequences of our choices.

When making decisions, it's easy to focus on immediate outcomes and gratification. However, the most impactful decisions are those that account for their long-term effects. But how does one shift their perspective to include long-term planning and impact?

This shift begins with looking beyond the present moment and visualizing the future implications of your choices. What seems like a good decision now may have different repercussions down the line. It's about aligning short-term goals with long-term visions.

As you navigate through this chapter, reflect on Alex's approach to community planning. His ability to look ahead ensured that the decisions made today would benefit the community for years to come.

To help you incorporate long-term thinking into your decision-making process, here are some guiding questions:

1. When making a decision, how often do you consider its impact five or ten years from now?
2. Can you think of a decision you made that had unforeseen long-term consequences?
3. How do you balance immediate needs with future goals?
4. What methods do you use to predict the potential long-term outcomes of your decisions?
5. How do your personal values influence your long-term planning?
6. In what ways can you ensure that your decisions are sustainable over time?
7. How do you assess the future impact of your decisions on others around you?
8. What role does adaptability play in your long-term planning?
9. How do you prepare for possible changes in circumstances that might affect your long-term plans?
10. What steps can you take to make more future-oriented decisions?

By the end of this chapter, like Alex, you will learn the importance of considering the long-term effects of your decisions. This perspective is crucial for making choices that are not only beneficial in the short term but also contribute positively to your future and the well-being of others.

Exercise #10

Practical Exercise:

Engage in 'Future Scenario Analysis'. Choose a current decision and project its outcomes into the future. Create scenarios for 1 year, 5 years, and 10 years down the line, considering both positive and negative impacts. This exercise will help you visualize the long-term implications of your choices.

Conclusion: Embracing Your Decision-Making Journey

As we reach the conclusion of this enlightening journey together, it's time to reflect on the key insights and transformations you've experienced. This book has been more than just a collection of chapters; it has been a pathway to enhancing your decision-making skills, a guide to understanding yourself better, and a companion in your journey of personal growth.

You've explored how to align decisions with your values, manage emotions, learn from the past, set effective goals, evaluate risks and rewards, seek diverse perspectives, handle uncertainty, improve problem-solving skills, build decision-making confidence, and consider the long-term impacts of your choices. These are tools not just for today but for a lifetime of confident and effective decision-making.

As you move forward, remember that decision-making is an evolving skill that benefits from continuous practice and reflection. Keep this book close; return to it whenever you find yourself at life's crossroads or when you need a reminder of your own capabilities and strengths.

Now, I'd like to extend my heartfelt gratitude to you for choosing this book. Your engagement and willingness to embark on this journey are what give life to these pages. If you've found value in this book, if it has touched your life or transformed your approach to decision-making, I kindly ask you to share your experience.

Leaving a review is more than just feedback for me; it's a way to help others who might be standing where you once were. Your review can shine a light on this book for someone else in need of guidance. It's your chance to pass on the wisdom and insights you've gained. Think of it as a way to contribute to a larger community of individuals all striving to make better, more informed decisions in their lives.

Your thoughts, reflections, and experiences are powerful. They have the potential to inspire, motivate, and encourage others. By sharing your review, you are not only supporting the continuation of this work but also helping to spread a message that could significantly impact the lives of others.

As we part ways in this book, remember that the journey of self-improvement and thoughtful decision-making does not end here. It is an ongoing process, one that you are now better equipped to navigate. Continue to grow, reflect, and make decisions that lead you to a life of fulfillment and purpose.

Thank you once again for joining me on this journey. Here's to making decisions that resonate with our deepest values and aspirations, and to a future where our choices reflect the best of who we are.

With gratitude and best wishes,
Yakalou!